THE
40-DAY FAST
Journal

A JOURNEY TO
SPIRITUAL TRANSFORMATION

WENDY SPEAKE

BakerBooks

a division of Baker Publishing Group
Grand Rapids, Michigan

Published by Baker Books
a division of Baker Publishing Group
PO Box 6287, Grand Rapids, MI 49516-6287
www.bakerbooks.com

Printed in the United States of America

ISBN 978-1-5409-0121-7

The author is represented by the William K. Jensen Literary Agency.

20 21 22 23 24 25 26   7 6 5 4 3 2 1

THIS JOURNAL BELONGS TO:

_____

DATES OF FAST:

_____ TO _____

WHAT I'M FASTING FROM:

_____

_____

_____

_____

HOW I HOPE TO SEE GOD MOVE
DURING THESE FASTING DAYS:

_____

_____

_____

_____

A SIMPLE PRAYER BEFORE I FAST:

Lord, You promise in Your Word that if I seek You with all my heart, I'll find You. What an invitation! You also say that when I seek Your kingdom and Your righteousness before all else, You'll add other good things to the blessing of Your nearness. I'm going to stop turning to false fillers these forty days in order to turn to You. Lord, prove Yourself true to Your Word. I humbly ask in Jesus's name, Amen.

But seek first his kingdom and his righteousness, and all these things will be given to you as well. (Matthew 6:33)

Transformed
by Forty Days of Fasting

THERE'S SOMETHING SPECIAL about the number forty, and there's something special about fasting. Put the two together and you have the opportunity to experience not only a physical hunger but a spiritual hunger as well! Whether you're fasting from sugar, social media, shopping, grains, alcohol, or all food until noon each day, this resource will help you stay focused on the transforming work of Christ in your life.

Author Rick Warren pointed out the power of forty days in the introduction to his book *The Purpose Driven Life*:

> The Bible is clear that God considers 40 days a spiritually significant time period.
> - Noah's life was transformed by 40 days of rain.
> - Moses was transformed by 40 days on Mount Sinai.
> - The spies were transformed by 40 days in the Promised Land.
> - David was transformed by Goliath's 40-day challenge.

- Elijah was transformed when God gave him 40 days of strength from a single meal.
- The entire city of Nineveh was transformed when God gave the people 40 days to change.
- Jesus was empowered by 40 days in the wilderness.
- The disciples were transformed by 40 days with Jesus after the resurrection.*

Use this journal to chronicle your own forty-day journey to transformation. Christlikeness is part of the sanctification process and deserves your full attention. When you're distracted by any number of things, fasting clears away distractions, giving you the focused time you need to be sanctified by God's Word (see John 17:17). Every entry in the journal begins with a place to record the Scripture you're meditating on that day. If you're using this book as a companion to *The 40-Day Sugar Fast* or *The 40-Day Social Media Fast*, then you'll already have a verse to jot down.

From there, communicate back to the Lord; tell Him what His Word and His Spirit are speaking into your life. Record the times you are tempted to turn to the things of this world instead of turning to the One who made the world. As you fast from distractions, intentionally grow your devotion to God.

Exchange your hunger for whatever it is you are fasting from for a holy hunger! Consume more of Christ and His Word, and let His abundant love transform you over the course of the next forty days!

---

* Rick Warren, *The Purpose Driven Life: What on Earth Am I Here For?* exp. ed. (Grand Rapids: Zondervan, 2013), 12.

FASTING

is merely denying
yourself something
temporary and ordinary
in order to experience

the One who is eternally

extraordinary.

Wendy Speake

day 1

The verse that spoke to me most today . . .

My response to God . . .

Whatever keeps me from my Bible is my enemy,
however harmless it may appear.

A. W. Tozer

day 2

The verse that spoke to me most today . . .

My response to God . . .

There are so many things that I mindlessly turn to each day—
so many things that I eat, read, watch, buy, and consume.
But God's invitation to His disciples was,
and remains, "Come to Me."

Wendy Speake

day 3

The verse that spoke to me most today . . .

My response to God . . .

Fasting detaches you from this world.
Prayer reattaches you to the next world.

Fulton J. Sheen

day 4

The verse that spoke to me most today . . .

My response to God . . .

Things which matter most must never be at
the mercy of things which matter least.

Johann Wolfgang von Goethe

day 5

The verse that spoke to me most today . . .

My response to God . . .

Five minutes of nibbling on a verse in the morning won't fill you up and fuel you through the other 1,435 minutes of the day. You need a continual feast to carry you through long fasting days.

Wendy Speake

day 6

The verse that spoke to me most today . . .

My response to God . . .

There is no neutral ground in the universe;
every square inch, every split second is claimed
by God and counterclaimed by Satan.

C. S. Lewis

day 7

The verse that spoke to me most today . . .

_____

_____

_____

My response to God . . .

_____

_____

_____

_____

_____

_____

_____

_____

_____

_____

_____

Fasting of the body is food for the soul.

John Chrysostom

Jesus Christ is not valued at all unless He is valued above all.

Augustine

day 8

The verse that spoke to me most today . . .

_____

_____

_____

My response to God . . .

_____

_____

_____

_____

_____

_____

_____

_____

_____

_____

_____

*Freedom in Christ is not freedom to do whatever you want;
it is for sure-footed self-reflection and for avoiding the
cultural bondage of sin. My freedom in Christ gives me
eyes to see that not all things are helpful for me, helpful
for others, or acceptable for my witness in the world.*

Tony Reinke

day 9

The verse that spoke to me most today . . .

_____

_____

_____

My response to God . . .

_____

_____

_____

_____

_____

_____

_____

_____

_____

_____

_____

Fasting gives me singularly happy afternoons.

Adalbert De Vogüé

day 10

The verse that spoke to me most today . . .

_____

_____

_____

My response to God . . .

_____

_____

_____

_____

_____

_____

_____

_____

_____

_____

_____

Human history [is] . . . the long terrible story of man trying to find something other than God which will make him happy.

C. S. Lewis

day 11

The verse that spoke to me most today . . .

My response to God . . .

If something other than God quickens your heart more than His love, take note. That which makes your heart beat fast may actually be the thing you need to fast from.

Wendy Speake

day 12

The verse that spoke to me most today . . .

My response to God . . .

The greatest enemy of hunger for God is not poison but apple pie. It is not the banquet of the wicked that dulls our appetite for heaven, but endless nibbling at the table of the world. It is not the X-rated video, but the prime-time dribble of triviality we drink in every night.

John Piper

day 13

The verse that spoke to me most today . . .

My response to God . . .

We abstain so that He might sustain.

Wendy Speake

day 14

The verse that spoke to me most today . . .

My response to God . . .

God made us to crave—to desire eagerly, want greatly, and long for Him. But Satan wants to do everything possible to replace our craving for God with something else.

Lysa TerKeurst

There is a God-shaped vacuum in the heart of every man which cannot be filled by any created thing, but *only* by God the Creator, made known through *Jesus Christ*.

Bill Bright

day 15

The verse that spoke to me most today . . .

My response to God . . .

Fasting is more about replacing than it is about abstaining—replacing normal activities with focused times of prayer and feeding on the word of God.

Gary Rohrmayer

day 16

The verse that spoke to me most today . . .

_____

_____

_____

My response to God . . .

_____

_____

_____

_____

_____

_____

_____

_____

_____

_____

Don't be afraid to get hungry;
be afraid of a life that never hungers for God.

Wendy Speake

day 17

The verse that spoke to me most today . . .

_____

_____

_____

My response to God . . .

_____

_____

_____

_____

_____

_____

_____

_____

_____

_____

Hearing God's voice has become the singular
quest of my heart, the sole pursuit that alone
satisfies the great longings of my heart.

Bob Sorge

day 18

The verse that spoke to me most today . . .

My response to God . . .

Whatever God is urging you to clear away cannot begin to be compared to what He ultimately wants to bring you.

Beth Moore

day 19

The verse that spoke to me most today . . .

My response to God . . .

Nothing heightens our physical and spiritual alertness like fasting. When I fast and pray, my ears are open to hear, my eyes are open to see, and my spirit is open to discern the things of God.

Wendy Speake

day 20

The verse that spoke to me most today . . .

_____

_____

_____

My response to God . . .

_____

_____

_____

_____

_____

_____

_____

_____

_____

_____

We are not human beings having a spiritual experience.
We are spiritual beings having a human experience.

Pierre Teilhard de Chardin

day 21

The verse that spoke to me most today . . .

_____

_____

_____

My response to God . . .

_____

_____

_____

_____

_____

_____

_____

_____

_____

_____

_What is it, then, that this desire and this inability proclaim to us,
but there was once in man a true happiness of which there now
remains to him only the mark and empty trace, which he in vain
tries to fill from all his surroundings, seeking from things absent
the help he does not obtain in things present? But these are all
inadequate, because the infinite abyss can only be filled by an
infinite and immutable object, that is to say, only by God himself._

Blaise Pascal

day 22

The verse that spoke to me most today . . .

_____

_____

_____

My response to God . . .

_____

_____

_____

_____

_____

_____

_____

_____

_____

_____

_____

I need God to consume me more than my life currently does.

Lisa Whittle

day 23

The verse that spoke to me most today . . .

My response to God . . .

You are missing the point entirely if you have found a way
to fast without experiencing hunger. Hunger pangs are a
holy tool, reminding us that we are fasting, why we are
fasting, and whom we want to be most hungry for.

Wendy Speake

LET YOUR
hunger pangs
become like
church bells
calling you to
prayer.

Bill Gaultiere

day 24

The verse that spoke to me most today . . .

_____

_____

_____

My response to God . . .

_____

_____

_____

_____

_____

_____

_____

_____

_____

_____

Quit playing, start praying. Quit feasting, start fasting. Talk less with men, talk more with God.

Leonard Ravenhill

day 25

The verse that spoke to me most today . . .

_____

_____

_____

My response to God . . .

_____

_____

_____

_____

_____

_____

_____

_____

_____

_____

_____

_____

_____

_____

_____

_____

_____

_____

_____

_____

_____

*The purpose of this fast is not to simply step away
from distractions but to exchange those distractions
for real-life devotion. To whet your appetite for God so
that you turn to Him—not online distractions, food,
alcohol, or anything else—to satisfy your hunger.*

Wendy Speake

day 26

The verse that spoke to me most today . . .

My response to God . . .

_____

_____

_____

_____

_____

_____

_____

_____

_____

_____

_____

_____

*When we fast we are saying that the cry of our
souls is greater than the cry of our stomachs.*

Tony Evans

day 27

The verse that spoke to me most today . . .

My response to God . . .

_Fasting as a religious act increases our sensitivity to
that mystery always and everywhere present to us. . . .
It is an invitation to awareness, a call to compassion
for the needy, a cry of distress, and a song of joy. It is a
discipline of self-restraint, a ritual of purification, and a
sanctuary for offerings of atonement. It is a wellspring
for the spiritually dry, a compass for the spiritually lost,
and inner nourishment for the spiritually hungry._

Father Thomas Ryan

day 28

The verse that spoke to me most today . . .

My response to God . . .

You can eat all the kale, buy all the things, lift all the weights, take all the trips, trash all that doesn't spark joy, wash your face and hustle like mad, but if you don't rest your soul in Jesus, you'll never find your peace and purpose.

Alisha Illian

day 29

The verse that spoke to me most today . . .

My response to God . . .

If I find in myself desires which nothing in this world can satisfy, the only logical explanation is that I was made for another world.

C. S. Lewis

day 30

The verse that spoke to me most today . . .

My response to God . . .

The purpose of [fasting] is to loosen to some degree the
ties which bind us to the world of material things and our
surroundings as a whole, in order that we may concentrate
all our spiritual powers upon the unseen and eternal things.

Ole Hallesby

If you don't feel strong desires for the *manifestation* of the glory of God, it is not because you have drunk deeply and are satisfied. It is because you have nibbled so long at the table of the world. Your soul is stuffed with small things, and there is no room for the great.

God did not create you for this. There is an appetite for God. And it can be awakened. I invite you to turn from the dulling effects of food and the dangers of idolatry, and to say with some simple fast: "This much, O God, *I want you*."

John Piper

day 31

The verse that spoke to me most today . . .

My response to God . . .

_Fasting confirms our utter dependence upon God by
finding in Him a source of sustenance beyond food._

Dallas Willard

day 32

The verse that spoke to me most today . . .

_____

_____

_____

My response to God . . .

_____

_____

_____

_____

_____

_____

_____

_____

_____

_____

Are the things you are living for worth Christ dying for?

Leonard Ravenhill

day 33

The verse that spoke to me most today . . .

My response to God . . .

Every time I have fasted I have found my worship experience sweeter, the illumination of God's Spirit brighter and the hunger for God's Word stronger.

Gary Rohrmayer

day 34

The verse that spoke to me most today . . .

My response to God . . .

Whatever is your best time in the day,
give that to communion with God.

Hudson Taylor

day 35

The verse that spoke to me most today . . .

_____

_____

_____

My response to God . . .

_____

_____

_____

_____

_____

_____

_____

_____

_____

_____

_____

Consider each Sabbath day a fasting day. A day to fast from work in order to rest, and to fast from constant connectedness with the world in order to connect with the One who made the world. Fasting is the key to Sabbath rest.

Wendy Speake

Sometimes
you have to
go fast
in order to
slow down.

Wendy Speake

day 36

The verse that spoke to me most today . . .

My response to God . . .

Fasting is abstaining from anything that hinders prayer.

Andrew Bonar

day 37

The verse that spoke to me most today . . .

My response to God . . .

The deepest level of communication is not communication
but communion. It is wordless. It is beyond words,
and it is beyond speech, and it is beyond concept.

Thomas Merton

day 38

The verse that spoke to me most today . . .

My response to God . . .

Christ is either Lord of all, or He is not Lord at all.

Hudson Taylor

day 39

The verse that spoke to me most today . . .

My response to God . . .

God doesn't want a temporary sugar sacrifice;
He wants a forever living sacrifice.

Wendy Speake

day 40

The verse that spoke to me most today . . .

My response to God . . .

Stay close to God and you won't go running after false gods again. Fill your life with the Spirit and you won't indulge the flesh.

Wendy Speake

We fast because . . .
we need to be sure
that we are saying
a firm goodbye to
everything
in us that still
clings to the old.

N. T. Wright

Life
beyond Your Fast

THE PURPOSE OF FASTING is always feasting. Just because your fast is over doesn't mean the feast has to be. Now that you've developed an appetite for the things of God—His sweet Presence and transforming Word—*keep seeking Him*. Though your fast is through, the feast should never be. Dive into the Word again today and tomorrow and the next day. Keep feasting!

If and when you forget to feast, fast again in order to remember.

Spend a few moments communicating with the Lord about what you learned and how you plan to stay close to Him now that your fasting days are over:

_____

_____

_____

_____

Instead of setting aside a season to fast, choose seasons not to fast. Take breaks from the intimate practice of fasting in order to spend more time enjoying the things of this world—rather than the other way around.

Wendy Speake

Wendy Speake is the author of *The 40-Day Sugar Fast* and *The 40-Day Social Media Fast*, and is coauthor of *Triggers: Exchanging Parents' Angry Reactions for Gentle Biblical Responses*. Wendy hosts her annual online 40-Day Sugar Fast every January and her 40-Day Social Media Fast every Lent. She lives in Escondido, California. Learn more at www.wendyspeake.com.

CONNECT WITH
Wendy

Discover more from Wendy at

WENDYSPEAKE.COM

or find her on Facebook or Instagram today.